CALIFORNIA STATE (1862)

The Hidden History of the CSU in San Jose and Beyond

MICHAEL HAROLD

California State (1862)

ISBN: 0615833233
ISBN-13: 9780615833231

Library of Congress Control Number: 2013910876
California State Press. San Mateo, CA

Cover Image: Front Side of Postcard of the State Normal School at San Jose campus in 1910 from the author's personal collection. The "State" in question is California, not San Jose.

ACKNOWLEDGMENTS

This book is dedicated to the most stalwart supporter of the CSU reform and restoration movement in San Jose, Mike Hentrich, who also edited this volume, and to my wife, Celina Wang, who has put up with more trips to the California State University, San Jose, campus than anyone who didn't attend that school should ever have to. I would also like to acknowledge all other supporters throughout the years, including most notably Pedro Aguilera and John Gillson. Also, special thanks to the University Special Collections staff at the Martin Luther King library that helped with the 2012 California State 150th Anniversary History exhibit and with sources and materials for this book.

CONTENTS

INTRODUCTION

On May 2, 2012, the state of California and the California State University (CSU) missed a once-in-a-lifetime opportunity to celebrate the 150th anniversary of the founding of the California State system of higher education. Instead, this significant anniversary was almost completely ignored by the state, the CSU, and the founding campus in San Jose.

What is now called the California State University was founded by the California State Legislature as the California State Normal School on May 2, 1862. After moving to San Jose and then spreading across the state, the normal schools later became the California State Colleges and, later still, the California State University.

One might think the 150th anniversary of this institution would be a momentous occasion for the State of California, the CSU and its founding campus in San Jose, worthy of recognition and perhaps even celebration. Incredibly, however, because of the hidden history and politics of the CSU and its founding campus in San Jose, the date went almost completely ignored and uncelebrated.

The reasons for this are complicated. Over the years the founding campus of the Cal State system gradually devolved from its grand original "California State" identity to its current more provincial "San Jose State" identity. But the malady of city-statism didn't stop there. It eventually spread to other campuses such as San Francisco State and San Diego State, and even to CSU-branded campuses such as Fresno State and Sacramento State.

Once this trend toward city-state identities had started, supporters of city-statism in San Jose were not content to control the current identity of the school. They took action to cover up the original Cal State identity, almost to the point of wiping it from history forever. For example, in 1957, after the school had recognized 1862 as its official year of establishment for almost 100 years, San Jose State supporters changed the founding year of the school from 1862 to 1857, without the consent of the California State Legislature. They celebrated the school's so-called centennial that year, helping to obscure the school's original California State identity, which is associated with the May 2, 1862 date.

The loss of a strong campus-based California State identity by the founding campus and the CSU system gave birth to what could be described as an academic and cultural tragedy for the state of California and its state university system. It disconnects both San Jose State and the CSU system from its original history and identity and reduces the system to a collection of glorified city colleges. It is a tragedy for the prestige and stature of the entire CSU system.

Just as a child who is denied any sense of his or her early history and identity may experience problems later in life, the rewriting of early Cal State history, and the loss of its original California State identity, has left the CSU without a strong identity as a prestigious system of higher learning. Instead, it remains an "Invisible Giant"—largely a collection of relatively obscure city-named state universities, lacking the prestige of schools like Washington State, Oregon State, and Arizona State.

The California State University identity remains largely co-opted by the CSU Chancellor's Office in Long Beach, where CSU employees are free to buy CSU-branded merchandise and apparel. Meanwhile, students and alumni at the oldest campuses have to settle for identities such as San Jose State and San Diego State and are denied the right to fully leverage their school's association with the CSU system in marketing their degrees.

This situation denies students and alumni the right to benefit from the name of the great state of California, arguably the best-known and most-loved state in the United States, perhaps even in the world. It also affects the prestige and development of the entire CSU system, which remains a disjointed collection of mostly city-oriented state universities without the unifying prestige of at least one strong California State namesake campus.

To combat this situation, the author of this book and other San Jose State students and graduates founded a movement in 2003 to restore San Jose State's broader and more prestigious identity as the oldest and original California State campus. However this movement has remained hampered by the historical mythology constructed by San Jose State supporters to support their provincial identity for the school.

The purpose of this book is to debunk those myths and to protect and preserve the history of the original California State campus from being completely obliterated by San Jose city-statism.

To this end, the next six chapters of this book are devoted to the history of California State in San Jose and beyond, while the remaining chapters are a commentary on the current situation and status of San Jose State and the CSU system. It is hoped this book will help level the playing field between those who have attempted to rewrite the founding California State campus out of history and those who believe that California, not San Jose, is the best state for the CSU's founding campus in San Jose.

AMERICA, SPAIN, AND THE LEGEND
OF CALIFORNIA

1

This is a book about the history and identity of the California State system of higher education and how the loss of that identity and its related symbols and history in San Jose has affected that campus and the entire CSU system. Therefore, it makes sense to start with the historical origins of the California and San Jose identities.

It is thought the name "California" is derived from a mythical island of the same name described in *Las Sergas de Esplandian*, an early sixteenth-century novel by Spanish author Garci Rodriguez de Montalvo. The island was described as being near the "terrestrial side of Paradise." When Spanish explorers discovered Baja California, they believed it to be an island and called it California after the fictional location. Explorers and mapmakers later extended the name to the rest of the area now known as California.[1]

Possibly the first European explorer to visit what is now the State of California was Juan Rodriguez Cabrillo, who discovered San Diego Bay in 1542. Although little explored at the time, Spain claimed what is now the State of California as part of the larger province of Las Californias. Nevertheless, Sir Francis Drake landed near Point Reyes, north of San Francisco Bay, and claimed the area for England in 1579.

Despite these claims, the area remained sparsely settled until the late eighteenth century when Spain began colonizing it to forestall other European claims to the region. The area was re-designated as part of Alta California (Upper California), which also included present-day Nevada, Arizona, Utah, and parts of Colorado and Wyoming. The Spanish planned a system of religious missions to help colonize the area, propagate the Catholic faith, and control the native population. The natives were used as a source or indentured labor for the missions.

The mission nearest to San Jose, Mission Santa Clara de Asis, was founded in 1777 on land now occupied by Santa Clara University. A system of towns, or pueblos, was then founded to support the Spanish colonial system, which included military bases known as presidios. Later that year, El Pueblo de San Jose de Guadalupe, named after the Catholic Saint Joseph, was founded in what is now the City of San Jose, about three miles southeast of Mission Santa Clara. Although the pueblo was ostensibly secular, the official intent was clearly that it should help support nearby missions.[2] In 1797, another nearby mission called Mission San Jose was founded in what is now Fremont.

The missions eventually owned much of the best land that was then suitable for cultivation and had the advantage of unpaid labor. The effect of the mission system on the native population has been described as "catastrophic" and resulting in "anthropological devastation."[3] Natives who ran away from the missions were hunted down by the Spanish military. In broader society, Protestants were forbidden from owning property and the Mexican Inquisition loomed as a threat to anyone who strayed from religious orthodoxy.

Forces were already at work, however, that would liberalize society and loosen the hold of monarchy and religion on California. After a long war, Mexico won its independence from Spain in 1821. Republican ideals bested monarchism and Mexico became a republic in 1824, but Catholicism remained the sole official religion. Alta California became the largest province in the newly independent nation of Mexico.

The Mexican government began the process of secularizing the missions in 1834, confiscating the property of the Catholic church and distributing it to the Californios, descendants of Spanish settlers. The natives were freed from servitude to the missions, although many fared little better left to their own devices in a foreign culture.

Despite its independence from Spain, the government of Alta California remained distant and corrupt, leading to continual rebellions, changes in government, and nascent California nationalism. In 1836, rebellious Californios, backed by American settlers, declared the sovereign nation of Alta California, but the uprising failed and the province remained a part of Mexico.[4]

The Mexican-American war broke out in 1846, largely as a result of the establishment of the Republic of Texas and its subsequent annexation by the United States. That conflict spilled over into Alta California, and the California Republic was declared in Sonoma the same year. The revolt was taken over by the US military, which helped defeat Mexican forces in California.

In 1849, the California Constitutional Convention voted to forbid slavery in the state, and adopted the intricate Great Seal of California, which was destined to play a role in the state's higher education system. After a brief period of military governorship, California was admitted to the Union in 1850 as a free (non-slave) state.

What had been a sparsely populated northern province of the Viceroyalty of New Spain, dominated by a distant absolute monarchy and its church, had become the state of California, with a constitution that guaranteed the separation of church and state. The stage was set for the establishment of what would become the California State system of higher education, today known as the California State University (CSU).

ESTABLISHMENT OF THE CALIFORNIA STATE NORMAL SCHOOL

2

By the late 1800s, many states had established what were then known as "normal schools," primarily for the education of teachers. What is now Arizona State University was founded as such a school.[5] The California State Legislature created the California State Normal School on May 2, 1862.[6] It later evolved into both the California State University system and its San José State University campus.

Although the act of the California State Legislature founding the school referred to the institution as the "Normal School of the State of California," it was commonly referred to as the "California State Normal School." The 1870 Act that moved the school to San Jose formalized the California State Normal School name.[7] The school was created when the state took over a normal school that educated San Francisco teachers in association with that city's high school system. This school was generally known as either the San Francisco Normal School or the George W. Minn's Evening Normal School.[8]

The school was originally intended to be a truly statewide institution. The act creating the normal school established a board of trustees who set a limit of sixty students "with at least one student from each county." Nevertheless, only five ladies and one gentleman appeared when the school opened its doors on July 21, 1862.[9] Later the school did in fact educate teachers from every county in the state.[10]

To provide some historical context, the California State Normal School was founded as the early part of American Civil War raged in the East. Although some Californians were known to harbor Confederate sympathies, the state of California entered the conflict on the side of the Union and contributed men and materiel to the war effort.

Figure 1 – An image of the second California State Normal School building in San Jose from the 1880s with darkly clad female students in the foreground.

In 1871, the school moved to Washington Square Park at Fourth and San Carlos Streets in San Jose, California, where it is still located. The original building at Washington Square Park was completed in 1872 but burned down on February 10, 1880. It was replaced by a second building in 1881. That same year, the California State Legislature created a "Branch State Normal School of California" in Los Angeles,[11] which later became the University of California, Los Angeles (UCLA).

An early version of the Normal School's seal featured an open book with laurel branches surrounded by the words "California State Normal School," similar to the seal shared by the University of California (UC) campuses. However, that version of the seal appears only on diplomas from the Normal School's earliest years. Later, the state bestowed a version of its Great Seal upon the Normal School in San Jose. The seal depicts the goddess Minerva surveying a bucolic scene from early California history. She is adorned with a Greco-Roman shield and spear. Crude early forms of the seal first appeared in school documents in the 1800s. As the state matured, so did its Great Seal, and those changes were reflected in the official seal of the California State Normal School in San Jose.

Figure 2 - An early version of the seal of the State Normal School at San Jose from a 1908 degree. It features the Great Seal of California and says "Established in 1862."

In 1881, the same year the State Normal School at Los Angeles was created, a bell was forged to commemorate the original California State Normal School campus in San Jose. The words and characters "California State Normal School A.D. 1881" were forged into the bell's iron shell. The bell still adorns the San Jose State campus today, where it is primarily known as the "Tower Bell."

Historical facts regarding the bell and its forging are not well known because San Jose State does not favor the "California State" name forged into the bell and therefore provides little information about its historical origins or significance on the school's website or elsewhere. The bell itself, however, indicates that it was forged in the state of New York for the California State Normal School.

In 1887, the California State Legislature omitted the word "California" from the two Normal School campuses, naming them "State Normal Schools."[12] It remains a mystery as to why the State of California chose to omit the word "California" from the name of the schools. Perhaps the answer lies in contemporaneous events such as the founding of the University of California at Berkeley by the California State Legislature in 1868, or the establishment of Stanford University by a powerful U.S. Senator and former California governor in 1889. The cornerstone for Stanford was laid in May of 1887, the same month as the California State Normal School's twenty-fifth anniversary.[13] Perhaps there is a connection between these events, although as yet no evidence has been uncovered to prove it.

After 1887, the official name of the San Jose campus was the "State Normal School at San Jose." Despite this identity, the school continued to be referred to as the "California State Normal School, San Jose" in annual school catalogs, diplomas, and other official documents.[14]

The school's athletic teams initially played under the "Normal" identity. However, they gradually shifted to the State Normal School (SNS) identity, as evidenced by images of the SNS football and basketball squads from this era. A recent historical display in the Martin Luther King Library at San Jose State featured a number of pieces of State Normal School memorabilia, including an "SNS" pennant.

Figure 3 - The State Normal School at San Jose football team in 1910. Some jerseys display a large "N" for the "Normal."

Until 1887, the State Normal School had only two campuses: one in San Jose and one in Los Angeles. Other State Normal Schools were established in Chico in 1887, San Diego in 1897, and eventually elsewhere throughout the state. With the exception of the Los Angeles campus and Santa Barbara campuses, the system of State Normal Schools would later become the California State University system. In 1919, the State Normal School at Los Angeles became the Southern Branch of the University of California, now the University of California, Los Angeles.

Around the time the Los Angeles campus went over to the UC system, city-state identities like "San Jose State" started to emerge at some of the Normal School campuses. These identities are generally based on the formula of the name of the campus home city plus the word "State." Perhaps this shift occurred because without the word "California" as part of its identity; the Cal State system experienced some difficulty in managing its "State Normal School" identity across several campuses.

THE STATE TEACHERS COLLEGES

3

In 1921, the California State Legislature decreed that the remaining State Normal Schools would be known as State Teachers Colleges, and that the original campus would be known as the "State Teachers College of San Jose."[15]

A heated debate arose at the San Jose campus in 1925 over the school's colors. An attempt was made by some students to change the school's traditional gold and white colors to purple and white. Blue and gold are the official state colors of California with blue representing the sky and sea and gold representing the state's abundant mineral resources. Tradition won the day, and the school decided to keep the California State-oriented colors. Blue was later added, making the school's official colors blue, gold, and white.[16]

Prior to 1925, the publicly promoted brand identity of the founding Cal State institution and its athletic teams included a variety of names such as "the Normal" and later the SNS. But the school was no longer either of those things and needed a new identity. Recognizing this need, the school organized a student vote to choose among several identities, including the "Spartans" and the "Golds."

The Golds name was undoubtedly linked to the school's primary official color. At the time, there was a "Spartan Knights" student group on campus. The Spartan identity bears a resemblance to the goddess Minerva's shield, helmet, and armor in the Great Seal of California, which was also the seal of the evolving State Teacher's College in San Jose. Needless to say, the Spartan identity won the election and has been with the school ever since.[17]

THE STATE COLLEGES

4

In 1935, the California State Legislature designated the State Teachers Colleges as "State Colleges" to be administered from the State Department of Education in Sacramento. For the first time, "San Jose" became the primary part of the founding campus' name: San Jose State College. Despite the name change, the state colleges were still primarily focused on educating teachers.[18]

In 1944, the California State system spawned its second UC campus when the California State Legislature transferred Santa Barbara State College to the University of California. That campus is now UC Santa Barbara.

In the late 1950s, the state colleges underwent a major expansion with new campuses being authorized in Fullerton, Hayward, Stanislaus, the San Fernando Valley, Sonoma, San Bernardino, and Dominguez Hills. Under the Donahue Higher Education Act of 1960, in 1961 the California State Colleges became a separate institution with its own board of directors.[19]

Contrary to descriptions on SJSU websites, San Jose State was a part of the California State system throughout these years and did not "join" the CSU at a later date. In fact, in 1957, California Governor Goodwin Knight called the San Jose campus "the keystone of the arch of the California State college tradition."[20]

REWRITING HISTORY AT SAN JOSE STATE

5

For almost one hundred years, the California State Normal School and its successor institutions used 1862 as the school's official year of establishment, as evidenced by the school's publications and seals during that time. For example, the 1919 California State Normal School catalog says "Established in 1862."

In the mid-1950s, however, the school's year of establishment was changed to 1857. Records in the SJSU Special Collections archives show that the change was made by a committee planning a centennial celebration for that year. The year 1857 was chosen because that is the year of establishment of the predecessor institution to the Cal State Normal School, the San Francisco Normal School. The records indicate that the centennial planners knew they were changing a date that had been established by the California State Legislature, but that they thought it was okay to change it without the legislature's consent.[21] The centennial planning records do not describe the rationale for changing the school's year of establishment. But one possible explanation is that 1857 helps obscure the school's original California State identity, which is disliked by many San Jose State supporters.

Figure 4 - This image of the 1904 California State Normal School catalog cover says "Established in 1862" and helps disprove two SJSU fallacies: that the school's name was changed to San Jose State in 1887, and that its year of establishment was 1857.

Similar schools with similar histories have not, however, changed their years of establishment. For example, the University of California, Berkeley, was derived from another school founded in 1848, but Berkeley still uses 1868, its date of charter by the State of California, as its official date of establishment.[22]

Ironically, the 1857 year still used by SJSU not only celebrates the establishment of a high school class rather than a college, but also celebrates a school that was never located in San Jose. Nevertheless, even after the school's 1957 "centennial," the school continued to recognize and celebrate its authentic year and date of establishment. For approximately six years in the late 1950s and early 1960s, the school celebrated "Founder's Day" in early May. This commemorates the May 2, 1862, establishment of the California State Normal School by the California State Legislature. Today, San Jose State still identifies some unspecified date in 1857 as its time of establishment and sells collegiate merchandise indicating 1857 as the school's year of establishment.

The year of establishment was not the only part of the school's history revised in this era. For the first time, histories of the school written by San Jose State historians started to revise key dates in the school's history. One example is the myth about the existence of the "San Jose State Normal School." In *Pioneers for One Hundred Years: San Jose State College, 1857–1957,* Benjamin Gilbert claims the 1887 act changed the name of the school to the "San Jose State Normal School."[23]

However, as cited earlier, the legislative record and the school's records from this era prove the name was actually changed to the "State Normal School at San Jose." The principle public identity of the school after 1887 was the "SNS" as indicated by images, artifacts and publications of the era. Nevertheless, the full California State Normal School, San Jose, name also continued to be used to some extent.

In fact, "San Jose State" did not become an official part of the school's identity until 1935 when the school was renamed San Jose State College. The fact that the school's fight song "Hail,

Spartans, Hail,",", which was written in 1933, never mentions "San Jose State" is evidence that it was not yet a central part of the school's identity even then.

Thus the development of the historical myth of the "San Jose State Normal School" was either a sloppy mistake by San Jose State historians or a deliberate attempt to obfuscate the school's original California State identity. If the later, the development of this mythology was probably motivated by a desire to reinforce the emerging "San Jose State" name to the exclusion of any counter-balancing Cal State identity.

The revision of the school's history goes well beyond a few history books published by San Jose State professors. Even historical images, publications and artifacts in the SJSU Special Collections university archives that are clearly from the California State Normal School or SNS eras are mislabeled as "San Jose State Normal School" or "San Jose Normal School" materials.

And not only history has been revised, so has one of the school's most fundamental and significant symbols. For more than one hundred years, the Cal State Normal School and its successors used a version of the Great Seal of California as the school's seal, signifying its close relationship with the State of California. Nevertheless, around the time San Jose State advocates changed the school's year of establishment to 1857, the school introduced a new seal with a depiction of Tower Hall in place of the Great Seal.

Figure 5 – The State Normal School at San Jose basketball team from 1910. The image shows the "SNS" acronym on the players' jerseys and even on the basketball, helping disprove the assertion that the school's identity was San Jose State at this time.

In summary, San Jose State supporters rewrote history by changing the school's year of establishment from 1862 to 1857, rewriting the Cal State Normal School out of the history books, replacing the school's historic Great Seal of California emblem, and mislabeling historical records and artifacts. In doing so, the evidence shows that San Jose State supporters have not only sought to control the current identity of the school but have also reached back in time to alter its history and many of its most significant symbols and traditions for political ends.

THE CALIFORNIA STATE UNIVERSITY—IN SAN JOSE AND BEYOND

6

In 1972, the state of California finally attempted to fully overturn its earlier removal of the word "California" from its state educational campuses. The California State Colleges were designated the California State University and Colleges. Fourteen of the campuses were renamed using the "California State University, name of city" model, with the exception of the two Cal State Polytechnic campuses, which retained those names. Five of the newer campuses remained colleges.[24]

This action followed the template set by the University of California and other public university systems: each campus is named for the statewide institution, followed by the name of the city in which the campus is located. For example, the founding UC campus is named the "University of California, Berkeley."

The act creating the CSU did away with the 1935 "San Jose State" name and, in 1972, the institution was renamed the "California State University, San Jose," an updated version of its original California State Normal School name.[25]

Despite a positive reception to this prestigious and nationally recognizable name by the university president and editorial writers at the *Spartan Daily* student newspaper, San Jose State supporters declared war on the restoration of the school's original identity. In their book Washington Square, Benjamin Gilbert and Charles Burdick write that, although the title was welcomed by some, the "alumni association refused to accept the legal title bestowed by law." They elaborated further that:

> A few individuals accepted the name change as beneficial, believing it would enhance the institution's image and give it more recognition beyond California's borders. It was argued that San Jose was not a state, and that the name California State University was proper; moreover, the new name was a return to the state institution's original name of 1862; when it was known as the California State Normal School.[26]

Sounding sympathetic to the California State name, Gilbert and Burdick observe that the majority "seemed to prefer the more provincial name." They add that the controversy over the name continued for almost two years.

While California State University, San Jose, was the official name, it was used in the official undergraduate and graduate bulletins, on the *Spartan Daily* masthead and on Spartan Shops apparel and merchandise. In fact, Spartan Shops ran an ad in the Spartan Daily declaring "SJSU Doesn't Exist," featuring CSU San Jose apparel and merchandise, and encouraging students to buy it.

Figure 6 - The cover of the California State University, San Jose Graduate Catalog for 1972-74.

Nevertheless, San Jose State supporters launched a campaign to downgrade the school back to the provincial "San Jose State" identity. The traditional practice at most campuses is that students would be allowed to vote on such a change. However, instead of allowing students and alumni to vote on keeping an identity that included both "California State" and "San Jose," the San Jose State Alumni Association went straight to the California

State Legislature where they pushed through a bill to downgrade the school's identity back to "San Jose State."

Supporters of provincial identities at a few other campuses also wanted similar reversions to their city-state names. As a result, the legislature passed a law that gave most campuses the right to choose either a California State or city-state name. The San Jose, San Francisco, San Diego, and Humboldt campuses were, however, required to revert back to the city-state name identity plus the word "university" or "college."[27] This resulted in names like "San Jose State University" that did not identify the schools as part of the broader California State University and Colleges system.

City-state identity proponents at California State University, Long Beach, attempted a similar reversion back to "Long Beach State," but were thwarted by that school's president, who recognized the value of an identity at least partially associated with the state of California. As a result, to this day that school enjoys a balanced city-state identity, which allows its students and alumni to choose between the Cal State Long Beach and Long Beach State identities.

A similar struggle between the city-state and California State identities has played out at Fresno State where, according to a professor's blog, the Academic Senate was approached in the 1990s with a proposal to change the official name from California State University, Fresno to Fresno State University. The professor recounts that "senator after senator" rose to denounce the proposal and reaffirm his or her support for a continued identification with the state of California.[28] It is also reported that Fresno State students have voted more than once not to change the school's name to FSU.

Former Fresno State football coach Pat Hill is said to have gone even further, advocating the Bulldogs assume the mantle of "California State" to raise the profile and prestige of that school and its athletic programs. Notwithstanding these preferences, the Fresno State administration introduced a new logo in 2012 eliciting howls of protest on university and other websites over the exclusion of the school's CSU identity from the new branding.

THE CALIFORNIA STATE
RESTORATION MOVEMENT
IN SAN JOSE

7

In 2003, San Jose State's football program was under siege from some of the school's professors who were pushing for its dissolution for financial reasons. This situation prompted heated discussions on athletic discussion boards like the SpartanThunder.com web site about how to improve the popularity and financial viability of Spartan athletics. Several participants in these discussions suggested restoring the school's original "California State" identity to broaden the appeal of the program. However, these suggestions were often met with furious denunciations by those who wanted to preserve only the San Jose State part of the school's tradition and were either ignorant of, or simply opposed to, its California State identity.

The argument for the CSU identity was that the San Jose State identity was simply too narrow and geographically restrictive to ever engender the kind of interest and support Spartan football needed to prosper. A number of participants pointed out that the San Jose State identity put Spartan football on the same level as smaller programs like Portland State or Sacramento State instead of on the level of bigger schools with equivalent histories like Washington State and Arizona State.

A participant in these discussions, the author of this book saw potential in the suggestions of these parties to restore San Jose's identity as the original California State campus. This observation prompted the launch of a movement to secure this goal. Initially, the movement focused on generating opinion and debate in the media and succeeded in having several articles and letters to the editor published in both the *Spartan Daily* and the *San Jose Mercury News.*

This action was followed by the launch of the Gostate.org website in early 2004, which included a shop called "The State Store" selling merchandise for CSU-oriented San Jose State students and alumni. Later that year, the author of this book established a California public benefit nonprofit association called the California State Alumni Association, Inc. (CSAA). Its goals include protecting and preserving the history of the founding Cal State campus in San Jose and the restoration its CSU identity and symbols for the benefit of the school, its alumni, students, and educators.

In early 2005 Alexander Gonzalez, president of the California State University, Sacramento (also known as "Sacramento State"), attempted to unilaterally change the name of that school to "Sacramento State University." However, the school's Academic Senate rose in defense of the CSU identity, citing its greater "gravitas" than just "Sac State." Gonzalez backed down, and the school retained a balanced city-state identity.[29] With the close of this affair, Sacramento State joined Long Beach State and Fresno State as CSU campuses that have fought to retain a CSU identity rather than to suppress it.

The schools where alumni have fought to suppress their CSU identities in the past include San Jose State, San Francisco State, San Diego State, Sonoma State, and Humboldt State. At some of these campuses, particularly San Jose State, the prevailing culture promotes a negative view of the school's CSU identity, despite the fact it remains a CSU campus. The commonly held belief is that the CSU brand is somehow cheapened by the fact that several other campuses share it. These feelings are so intense among some SJSU alumni it could be argued that San Jose State promotes dislike of the CSU. As evidenced by countless online discussions, some San Jose State supporters bristle with hostility when confronted with the fact that not all alumni share these views.

Notwithstanding this opposition, the CSU restoration movement in San Jose, inspired by the uprising of the pro-CSU professors at Sac State, began to focus on more concrete political actions to achieve its goals. In 2006, the author of this book met with a committee of SJSU's Associated Students (A.S.) student government to propose an "alternate identity" for the school similar to that in place at CSU Long Beach. Under such an identity, both the San Jose State name and an identity including the words "California State University" would coexist, as is the case at several CSU campuses. Surprisingly, the committee enthusiastically endorsed the proposal. But it was later crushed by A.S. President Rachel Greathouse, according to committee members.

Denied the opportunity to advance the cause via student government, CSU identity supporters decided to go straight to the students. In 2007, led by MBA student Mike Hentrich and the author of this book, they collected more than 150 student signatures to have the issue of a CSU alternate identity for San Jose State put on the annual student ballot.[30]

By this time, the movement for a restored CSU identity had moved beyond focusing primarily on the benefit of a broader identity for Spartan athletics and had begun to focus more on the benefit of a CSU identity for students and graduates marketing their educational experience and looking for jobs.

Despite the fact that the students clearly met all requirements for a student vote, some SJSU officials objected to the initiative and attempted to delay it until the deadlines for its implementation had passed. This move led the author of this book, a former practicing attorney, to step in and appeal to other school administrators for help and to threaten legal action in defense of the initiative. Fortunately, other school officials interceded and allowed the initiative to proceed to a vote.

Figure 7 - A logo created in support of the CSU Restoration Initiative at San Jose State in 2007 shows how easily the school's city and state identities could be combined.

With the vote scheduled for March 2007, despite claiming neutrality, SJSU officials campaigned against the initiative.[31] In social media websites, students also accused the SJSU Spartan Squad of a campaign of disinformation against the initiative. The Spartan Squad was trying to convince students it was a total name change rather than just an alternate identity that would restore a CSU affiliation while preserving the San Jose State name. The SJSU Alumni Association even got involved, passing a resolution condemning the initiative and reiterating its support for the San Jose State-only identity.

The text of the initiative voted on by students was as follows:

Shall the State of California and/or the CSU Trustees restore the rights of students at San Jose State to identify with the State of California and the CSU, and to market their educational experience under the CSU name by:

(1) Restoring a publicly promoted CSU identity at San Jose State that includes the words "California State University" while also maintaining the "San Jose State" identity (e.g., San Jose State-CSU San Jose), and

(2) Restoring the rights of San Jose students to purchase apparel, gear and accessories from the University and its licensees that include the words "California State University", while maintaining the right to purchase "San Jose State" products?

Despite efforts by SJSU administrators and supporters to delay, defeat, and spread disinformation about the initiative, 606 students voted for it, comprising 25 percent, or one of every four students voting. The *Spartan Daily* also reported that polling administrators advised students how to vote yes or no on the "name change,"[32] which over-simplified the issue and probably affected the outcome.

After the initiative, supporters filed written complaints with the university about the effort to prevent the student vote, together with a California Freedom of Information Act request for all documents related to such actions. A number of emails and other communications were delivered in response to the request, and shortly thereafter a senior administrator's employment with the university came to an end. Inquiries with the university as to whether the two events were connected were not answered.

Despite the defeat of the initiative, the CSAA pressed on, building its presence on the web and in social media groups on Yahoo and Myspace and later LinkedIn and Facebook, among others.

In 2010, the CSAA submitted a formal application to become a chapter of the SJSU Alumni Association. The application was supported by two meetings with the Alumni Association during which the CSAA was represented by three alumni in each meeting. In the second meeting, the CSAA was allowed to make a presentation describing the potential power of the school's identity as the founding California State campus and setting out the case for collaboration between the two groups. Despite these cordial meetings, then SJSU Alumni Association President Rachel Greathouse denied the chapter application. The CSAA attempted to appeal the decision to the alumni association's entire board of directors, citing that organization's responsibilities under state and federal law as a recipient of government-funded educational resources. The SJSU Alumni Association denied the appeal, claiming that its use of such resources did not make it a "state actor."

Later, the CSAA made an appeal for help in securing CSU alumni rights at San Jose State to the CSU Alumni Council and to the CSU Legal Department. Despite the existence of provisions in California educational law that guarantee the right to use the CSU name and prohibit domination of state institutions by political groups like San Jose State supporters, the appeals fell on deaf ears.

In 2012, the CSAA also attempted to get both the CSU and San Jose State to recognize the 150th anniversary of the founding of the California State Normal School on May 2, 1862. Having instead celebrated San Jose State's purported 150th anniversary in 2007, they both refused to recognize the anniversary date established by the California State Legislature.

Most recently, the CSAA cosponsored a historical exhibit in association with SJSU Special Collections in the Martin Luther King Library at San Jose State. The exhibit featured photographs and memorabilia organized into five subsections: The California State Normal School, the original 1862 year of establishment, the Great Seal of California/San Jose State, the California State Bell (aka the Tower Bell), and the California State University, San Jose. With the kind assistance of Special Collections Director Danelle Moon, the exhibit, which was scheduled to run for just a few months in early 2012, was extended for most of the year.

Figure 8 - The California State Normal School bell, which features the engraved words "California State Normal School A.D. 1881". Although it still graces the oldest Cal State campus in San Jose, since the image was taken it has been badly vandalized and moved under a tree where it will probably deteriorate more quickly.

After the exhibit, the CSAA requested that permanent special collections on the Cal State Normal School, the 1862 year of establishment, and CSU San Jose be established. The group also requested that blatant mislabeling of Cal State Normal School and SNS publications, photographs and artifacts as being from the mythical "San Jose State Normal School" be corrected. The CSAA has also asked SJSU Professor Annette Nellen and others to correct misleading information on the San Jose State web site regarding the school's identity at various times. As of publication of this book, none of these requests has been honored. As described above, the main SJSU web site and the SJSU Special Collections web site continue to offer false and misleading information about the school's identity over the years.[33]

Today, the CSAA has a three-person board of directors, has regular meetings and events, maintains a website at www.csualumni.org, and hosts social media groups on LinkedIn, Facebook, Classmates. com, Yahoo Groups and other sites that comprise more than 2,250 members.

This concludes the section of this book devoted to California State higher education history. The remaining chapters analyze how these historical developments and other factors have affected San Jose State and the Cal State system in the modern era, and how reform of these institutions can benefit the CSU in San Jose and beyond.

CALIFORNIA STATE VS. SAN JOSE STATE

8

SJSU supporters often dismiss the controversy over the school's identity as unimportant, saying it would have no impact on the future of the school. At the same time, they steadfastly defend the school's San Jose-only identity. This confusing response calls into question their honesty, for if the school's identity is not important, why strongly defend one name against another?

Also, despite the San Jose State University name, the advertising slogan "SJSU Doesn't Exist" used by Spartan Shops during the CSU San Jose era still has validity. There is no legal institution called San Jose State University. The San Jose campus is part of a statewide corporate entity called the "Trustees of the California State University."[34] Even current San Jose State degrees indicate that they are officially granted by "The Trustees of the California State University at San Jose."

CSU restoration supporters see the right to use this identity as a civil rights and freedom of speech issue related to the prestige of their school, the value of their degrees, and their right to market their educational experience as they see fit. After all, what is more important to college graduates than the prestige, value, and marketability of their degree and their ability to find a job with it? If graduates believe they gain a competitive advantage by being able to identify their school as the founding California State campus without having to explain it why should they be prevented from doing so? CSU-oriented alumni see their right to a California State-branded school and degree as a property right, bought and paid for with their tuition and taxes. These funds are paid to the state of California, not the city of San Jose.

Another issue is the question of fairness. Should SJSU supporters be able to get away with rewriting the school's history for the sake of maintaining their control? An academic institution is supposed to support intellectual honesty and fairness rather than academic dishonesty and historical revisionism for political ends.

Also, the lack of at least one campus with a strong California State-identity affects the system far beyond the San Jose campus. In 1971, Donald Gerth and James Haehn noted the lack of name recognition of the California State Colleges system in the title of their book: *An Invisible Giant: The California State Colleges.*[35]

Even today the CSU system remains an invisible giant to some degree because it lacks a namesake campus, the role usually played by the oldest school in a system. The namesake gives the university system a sense of history, identity, tradition, and meaning. This often finds its most potent expression during the football season. The oldest UC campus, Berkeley, plays this role for the UC system with its "California" identity.

The CSU identity remains largely co-opted by the CSU Chancellor's Office in Long Beach, where administrators call themselves "The California State University" even though they are not a campus. These administrators are free to buy CSU-branded merchandise and apparel and have even adopted a "school" color (red), which alienates real CSU campuses with other colors. Meanwhile, students and alumni at the older campuses are stuck with provincial identities like "San Jose State" and are denied the right to fully leverage their school's association with the CSU system.

Frequent contacts with administrators from the CSU Chancellor's office also call into question their objectivity on the issue. The Chancellor's office is dominated by graduates of CSU Long Beach and other southern California campuses. These officials seem all too willing to dismiss the concerns of CSU-oriented alumni at San Jose State. Meanwhile, they launch programs that help the CSU Chancellor's office, and its southern California campuses assume the mantle of the CSU and become more prominent. An example of this situation is the recent launch of the "Cal State Online" program, which is run exclusively by the Chancellor's office for the benefit of mostly southern California campus like by CSU Fullerton and Dominguez Hills.[36]

SJSU supporters justify the "San Jose State" identity by pointing out that it is different from the name used by some other CSU campuses. Unique is better they say, and they don't want the school to have a "generic" identity similar to other CSU campuses. There are too many CSU-named campuses, they say.

The counter-argument is threefold: First, unique is not always good. The Edsel automobile's name was unique, but was it a good car? Secondly, is "San Jose State" truly that unique? It's very similar to Saint Joseph's University, San Jose City College,

San Francisco State, San Diego State, and many other "city-state" named schools across the country. Thirdly, San Jose's identity as the original and oldest California State institution of higher learning is also unique. No other campus in the world can claim that distinction. Moreover, UC Berkeley shares the University of California part of its name with nine other campuses but is hardly considered generic.

Critics of the school's CSU identity also point out that "CSUSJ" is an overly long and ugly acronym. Although "SJSU" isn't that beautiful either, this point has some merit. Part of the problem is that the city of San Jose has a two-word name. The letter "J" is also an odd letter in that it faces backward instead of forward. The solution to this problem is simple: the school should not use the "CSUSJ" acronym, using other variants like "California State," "Cal State," "CSU San Jose," or "Cal State San Jose" instead. After all, UC Berkeley is almost never referred to as "UCB."

SJSU supporters also point to "tradition" in maintaining the San Jose State-exclusive identity, saying the name has been that way for many years. CSU restoration supporters counter that the "California State" identity is an equally valid and important part of the school's tradition. It was the school's official name from its founding in 1862 to 1887, part of its unofficial name until 1921, part of the school's identity as a California State College, its official name again from 1972–1974, and part of its identity as a CSU campus ever since. Moreover, all subsequent Cal State campuses and the entire CSU Chancellor's Office itself sprang from the San Jose campus, so why shouldn't the school capitalize on its prestige as the founding campus of the entire system?

Figure 9 – Two vestiges of a hidden identity. A Cal State University San Jose pennant from the 1972-74 era, and a pennant from the Cal State College period that just says "San Jose" with the San Jose State College emblem featuring the Great Seal of California and "1862".

Clearly, SJSU supporters have the upper hand in the debate, having been able to defeat all attempts at reform since 2003. Although the San Jose State identity has its supporters, significant numbers of students and alumni believe the school would be better off with its original California State identity, symbols and traditions. For example, a restricted search on Google in May 2013 for the exact term "California State University, San Jose" reveals more than 62,000 results, the majority of which are people using that term to identify their degrees on their resumes and elsewhere.[37] It is incredible that so many people are using an identity that was been officially proscribed for almost 40 years. But it is not surprising. It is logical that an identity that evokes a much larger and well-known political entity like the state of California is preferred by many.

For example, even non-alumni outside of San Jose might be interested in California State-branded athletics because it represents their state. This phenomenon can be seen in states like Oregon and North Carolina where the athletics of the schools that share those state's names are a point of interest throughout those states. The Oregon vs. Oregon State rivalry is even called "Civil War" and often draws in state residents who did not attend either school.

In fact, at least two campuses around the country have recently upgraded themselves to evoke state identities rather than a narrower name tied to a city or smaller part of a state. Southwest Texas State University recently upgraded itself to Texas State University, San Marcos, and the former Mankato State University is now Minnesota State University, Mankato. In a similar move to represent a larger region, CSU Hayward changed its name to California State University, East Bay in 2005.

WHAT'S WRONG WITH
SAN JOSE STATE?

9

Based on almost ten years of feedback from hundreds of students and alumni, the following is a summary of what most dislike about the San Jose State identity.

For starters, it has a provincial and small-time sound to it, which many believe focuses too much on the city of San Jose. The name also fails to identify the school's location in California or its intimate relationship with the state as the founding Cal State campus. The school's relationship with the CSU system can be explained in a job interview, but in the competitive job market, applicants may never get the chance. Even if they do, it is better not to have to explain it.

Part of the problem is the city of San Jose itself. It claims to be the tenth largest city in the United States, but its urbanized center is relatively compact, making it seem like a smaller town. Most of San Jose's residents live in its sprawling 176-square mile hinterlands, far removed both physically and spiritually from the moribund and redevelopment-resistant downtown where San Jose State is located. By contrast, the city of San Francisco encompasses only about forty-seven square miles. In fact, San Jose's relatively small urban area would make it an ideal college town for a major California State University football school, drawing interest and support from the entire state, not just the city of San Jose.

Moreover, San Jose is not nearly as well known as other California cities like San Francisco, San Diego, and Los Angeles. In fact, in the recent *America's Favorite Cities 2012* survey by *Travel and Leisure Magazine,* those three cities ranked well, but San Jose was not mentioned at all.[38] As a result of San Jose's relative obscurity, the CSAA has heard complaints from alumni around the world that it is easier to market a Cal State-branded degree than a San Jose State-branded one. Alumni from many countries and backgrounds have also objected to the fact that it is sometimes necessary to explain that the school is located in the United States.

Indeed, there are many other cities, towns, and places named San Jose around the world the location of San Jose State can be confused with, most notably in Costa Rica, Mexico, Chile, and the Philippines, but also in Arizona, New Mexico, Texas, and Illinois. In fact, according to the US GEOnet server database, San Jose is the most commonly used place name in the world,[39] largely as a result of aggressive Spanish Catholic colonization of the world.

Possibly as a result of these and other factors, San Jose State also has a reputation for academic and athletic mediocrity. Every year, SJSU touts its ranking as one of the best schools in the *U.S. News & World Report* annual ranking of schools. But the school fails to mention that this is just a western regional ranking, which is secondary in prestige to the two hundred or so nationally ranked schools. In fact, even San Jose State's regional ranking is mediocre: as of early 2013 it was thirty-eighth among western universities.

So, if you add back in the national schools, SJSU is in fact tied for 238th place with the other regional universities in their regions. This is well behind nearby nationally ranked state schools such as UC Berkeley (#21), UCLA (#24), Oregon (#115), Washington State (#125), and Arizona State and Oregon State (both #139). It is also behind nearby western-region schools such as Santa Clara (#2) Cal Poly (#6), CSU, Long Beach (#28), CSU Chico and CSU Fullerton (both #31), and Cal Poly, Pomona (#34).[40]

Superior rankings for Cal State identity schools undercut the argument that SJSU's "unique" identity puts it above the CSU-named campuses. As a former student and graduate teaching assistant in the SJSU College of Business, the author of this book can attest that such rankings are not merely public relations. While there were some fine professors at the school, others seemed to be merely going through the motions of teaching. In addition, many senior students struggled with basic writing and other skills, despite the fact that they were close to graduation.

SJSU usually doesn't fare much better in rankings for the big-time NCAA sports like football and men's basketball where most years it ranks near the bottom of the 119 or so top division teams. Even in years when Spartan football does better, Spartan Stadium is mostly empty. For example, in the 2012 football season, SJSU managed for the first time in years to have a winning season. Yet attendance at home games averaged only 10,789 in a stadium built for more than 30,000, according to SJSU's own statistics.[41]

Perhaps one of the reasons for this mediocrity is the fact that SJSU is mostly a commuter school serving the San Jose metro area. According to SJSU's own website, historically only 8 percent of the school's students have lived on campus; the rest are commuters. SJSU attributes this residency to the school's "urban setting," but CSU-oriented alumni instead attribute it to the provincial San Jose State-only identity, which tends to attract commuters who live in the San Jose area. A possible consequence of this commuter-school status is that the campus area leaves much to be desired. It is ringed with "a multitude of halfway and sober living homes" for alcoholics, people with mental disabilities, and those recently released from jail.[42] As a result, the area can seem creepy and dangerous at times, with SJSU students often referring to it as being "ghetto."

Part of the problem has been SJSU's own policies of favoring local students with lower grades. Although this tendency does open educational opportunities for locals, it also discriminates against better students from other parts of the state and lowers academic standards for the whole school. SJSU reluctantly agreed to modify this policy starting in the fall of 2013, although some locals will continue to get preferences despite poorer grades. The local preference thus tends to hurt the school's academic reputation and buttress San Jose State provincialism at the campus.

Even some SJSU administrators seem to agree the SJSU identity makes recruiting residential students from elsewhere more difficult. For example, in a Nov. 3, 2004, article on former Academic Provost Marshall Goodman, the *Spartan Daily* wrote that: "When Goodman travels to other states to recruit for SJSU he said he may have to explain what SJSU is, 'but people know California—they just get it.'" Goodman's tenure as provost ended shortly after the article was published.

Then there is the religious issue. "Jose" is Spanish for "Joseph," who in the Christian tradition is the husband of Mary, the mother of Jesus Christ. Certain Christian denominations like Eastern Orthodoxy, Catholicism, and Anglicanism recognize "saints," and "San" is Spanish for saint. Thus "San Jose" stands for "Saint Joseph" in English. As previously mentioned, San Jose was originally named by Spanish colonialists who imposed a system of state-mandated Catholicism on the residents of California. Although these religions certainly have the right to their beliefs, it seems inappropriate that a U.S. state-funded public university's identity starts with the name of any religious figure.

According to a 2012 study by the Pew Research Center, the segment of the US population that claims no religious affiliation stands at close to 20 percent and is the fastest growing segment of the US population.[43] The religious name issue may be particularly acute for secular students and alumni who do not adhere to any religious faith and do not want to be saddled with a degree from a school with a religious-sounding name.

Moreover, the First Amendment to the United States Constitution mandates the separation of church and state. This amendment has been interpreted many times to prohibit state support of religious activities, displays, names, and identities. One could argue the San Jose-exclusive identity violates this mandate.

San Jose State is also located in the heart of Silicon Valley, the technology capital of the world where rational thinking, science, and technology are highly valued. In this arena, the San Jose State identity seems particularly outdated to some.

One CSU alumni supporter recently commented that the name seems "so 100 years ago."

But even if one doesn't accept that the name San Jose State University (Saint Joseph State University in English) is religious, the issue of a quasi-religious identity at San Jose State interfering with California State patriotism remains. A recent article in *Psychology Today* summarizing several academic studies postulated that enthusiasm for sports teams is replacing religion for many Americans.[44] State patriotism is a similar force, and if it were to be classified as a kind of secular religion its seminaries would be the state universities.

Evidence of this can be seen on autumn days at major public schools like Michigan, Ohio State, or California where the faithful gather to support their teams with fanatical, almost religious devotion. At these schools the name of the state and the school are fused. It's no longer just UC Berkeley, it's "California." Fans rightly support their states and their state universities in fervent displays of state/school patriotism. This devotion amounts to a kind of secular religion in support of these states and their beloved namesake schools. This in turn benefits the faithful by rewarding them with well-known, loved, and respected campuses that become nationally known.

At San Jose State, the rightful recipient of such devotion should be "California State," meaning both the state that founded and maintains the school and the school itself. Instead, SJSU supporters have effectively outlawed California State patriotism and subverted it to focus solely on the city of San Jose. However, San Jose is only the location of the school, not the political entity that founded, developed, funds, and maintains the school. Therefore, this devotion is largely misplaced.

Maintenance of the San Jose State identity could be said to equate to unlawful state support of two local identities to the exclusion of all others. The first is the old world-sounding identity that evokes the name of a Catholic saint and harkens back to the days when San Jose was founded to support Spanish colonialism and the mission system. The second is a kind of secular religion of city-statism that outlaws an attachment to the school's real benefactor, the State of California, and channels whatever devotion and support it can muster to a legally nonexistent entity called "San Jose State."

It should be noted, however, that CSU-oriented alumni do not disparage San Jose's Spanish heritage and do not want to change the name of the city of San Jose itself. Nor do they want to get rid of the school's city identity completely. CSU restoration advocates, who come from many cultural backgrounds, simply believe that a more balanced identity that includes *both* the school's state and city identities would be more equitable and beneficial for all students and alumni. After all, the word California is also derived from Spanish culture. Far from being anti-San Jose, the CSU restoration movement seeks to elevate San Jose's status in California and help revitalize its downtown area.

In summary, SJSU's academic failures, its lack of a respected brand, and its inability to field successful athletic teams creates resentment among many students and alumni. The school has a decidedly mediocre approval ranking of 3.5 on the popular review site *Yelp*, compared to 4.5 for UC Berkeley; Washington State; and CSU Long Beach; and 4.0 for Oregon State. One reviewer even called San Jose State a "glorified community college."[45]

HOW WOULD A RESTORED
CSU IDENTITY HELP?

10

Many believe the price paid by the founding CSU campus and its students and alumni for the San Jose State identity has been significant. Instead of becoming a statewide or even national power in academics and athletics, the school has declined into a commuter-oriented city college. It has a mediocre academic reputation and is unable to compete against nearby schools with similar histories like UC Berkeley, Washington State, Oregon State, and Arizona State.

This is far from a frivolous issue for many Spartans who graduate and struggle to find a good job or any job at all in the ultra-competitive Silicon Valley job market. The LinkedIn profiles of many SJSU alumni tell the story—many have either no job or only a marginal position they probably could have gotten without a degree. On their athletic discussion forums, Stanford alumni seem to enjoy emphasizing the struggles of SJSU grads, describing them as "sisters of the poor" and by other epithets. SJSU alumni who leave Silicon Valley are also faced with the issue of the relative obscurity of their school outside the South Bay region.

Of course, even partial restoration of a California State identity would directly address the issue of identifying the school as a CSU campus and its location in California. It would also dilute the issue of the school's religious identity, giving alumni and students at least a partially secular identity under which to market their degrees. That identity would at last be focused on the rightful subject of the school's gratitude: California State rather than San Jose State.

Many believe a restored CSU identity, given time, would also help the school evolve away from its limited commuter school reputation to become a better recognized state university. After all, "California State" is a much broader shared experience than San Jose State. California is the most populous state and possibly the best-known state in the United States, with some 38 million inhabitants. By comparison, San Jose claims fewer than one million residents in its sprawling territory. There are many more people with reason to identify with California State than there are with San Jose State.

To dismiss the CSU restoration proposal as a mere "name change" doesn't do it justice. What the CSAA proposes is more like a paradigm shift in the way the San Jose campus perceives and markets itself, both academically and athletically. It includes restoring "California State" as a part of the school's identity, restoring its 1862 year of establishment, restoring the school's historic Great Seal, and building a stronger and more supportive relationship with the state of California and other CSU campuses. This change would be a major shift away from San Jose-only provincialism that attempts to minimalize the school's association with the state at every turn. Instead, the school would embrace and exploit its relationship with the state of California as its oldest public institution of higher learning.

CSU restoration could also set up a number of promotion and tourism opportunities for the school and city that are non-existent under the SJSU identity. For example, California State-branded football could be marketed not just to San Jose State students but to those from other regional Cal State campuses such as East Bay, Monterey Bay, San Francisco, and Stanislaus, and even to Californians in general.

The school could turn the May 2 founding date of the Cal State system into an annual statewide celebration centered in San Jose. It could erect a California State monument on the campus, open a California State Institute, history museum and alumni house, and launch a Cal State history tour of the campus area. None of these ideas, however, would work under the SJSU identity simply because it has too few strong supporters, and little appeal to non-alumni outside of San Jose.

Change will not come easily, though. As described above, San Jose State supporters have already undone the restoration of the school's California State identity, changed the school's 1862 year of establishment, abandoned its historic Great Seal, and even compromised historical records and artifacts. These efforts amount to the development of a creation mythology for San Jose State. The school's indoctrination of its students in these areas is so pervasive that many SJSU alumni accept this mythology without question. Moreover, the use of the 1857 year of establishment has even spread to the CSU Chancellor's Office where its use makes a mockery of the CSU's Latin slogan *Vox Veritas Vita,* which means "speak truth as a way of life."

Figure 10 - A photo of San Jose State's Great Seal of California emblem taken in Tower Hall in 2004. For the most part, San Jose State no longer uses this beautiful and historic seal.

San Jose State supporters have blunted all attempts at democratic change and reform at the school. For example, the 2007 Initiative for a balanced city-state identity at the school was almost blocked by SJSU administrators, and then defeated by a disinformation campaign.

The SJSU Alumni Association later blocked an attempt by the CSAA to become a CSU-oriented alumni chapter.

California educational law provides that there can be only one state-supported alumni association per campus, but the SJSU alumni association appoints its own directors and officers, so there is no mechanism for new ideas or change to occur at the alumni level.

The current alumni association has failed to engage the overwhelming majority of San Jose State alumni. For example, according to the 2011/2012 CSU Annual Philanthropic Report, the SJSU Alumni Association represents only 11,891 or about 6 percent of the 194,878 addressable graduates of the school. The number giving donations is even smaller: only 4,144 or 2 percent of alumni.[46]

Another measure of the relative lack of support for SJSU is the size of its endowment. Even after a major fundraising effort called "Acceleration," the school's endowment is relatively small compared to other nearby public schools with similar backgrounds. According to U.S. News & World Report, the recent endowment values for four western public universities are as follows:[47]

SCHOOL	ENDOWMENT
University of California, Berkeley	$3.2 billion
Arizona State University, Tempe	$515 million
Oregon State University	$403 million
San Jose State University	$75 million

What separates SJSU from these schools is that they have been able to leverage the power of their state identities to build national rankings and strong residential student populations. These students bond more effectively with their schools and give more generously. SJSU, on the other hand, attracts mostly commuters, many of whom do not seem to identify with the school strongly or give to the school generously. This, in turn, has a negative impact on the school itself, which is not as able as other major state universities to afford the best educators and educational facilities.

Despite San Jose State's overwhelmingly anti-CSU policies, minor successes have been won. For example, a major school at the university, International and Extended Studies (IES), at least until recently identified itself in marketing materials as "The California State University Campus in Silicon Valley." In 2005, San Jose State's home jerseys for Spartan basketball sported the "STATE" brand many CSU supporters would like to see the school use more frequently, as did Spartan baseball uniforms in 2012.

Moreover, after deleting the California State Normal School page on Wikipedia twice and petitioning again for its removal, San Jose State supporters have since ceased their attack on the page and allowed it to exist. It has been integrated with the California State University and San Jose State pages and appears to have influenced the accuracy of their historical timelines. In 2011, after many contacts with CSU restoration advocates from San Jose, the CSU Chancellor's office launched a new Facebook page, called "Proud California State University Alumni" featuring a royal blue color scheme rather than the bright red "CSU color" they usually use.

Despite these minor successes, CSU-oriented students and alumni remain an ostracized group at San Jose State, forbidden from effectively marketing their degrees under the California State University name. They are not allowed to participate in official alumni affairs as a CSU-branded chapter and are prohibited from buying CSU-branded merchandise at the school store.

To truly integrate CSU-oriented alumni into the San Jose State community, university administrators should apply a fundamental principle of marketing and "segment" school supporters. As discussed above, there are tens of thousands of alumni using "California State University, San Jose" to market their degrees. This is despite the fact that this identity is outlawed, and they have to explain what school they mean. And there here are more than 2,200 students and alumni in CSU-oriented groups at San Jose State.

If school administrators really want to build support for the school, they must recognize that many students and alumni strongly prefer the school's identity as the oldest and original Cal State campus. Just as UC Berkeley uses both its "California" and "Berkeley" identities, SJSU should separate its state and city identities and allow students, graduates, educators, donors and other supporters the freedom to identify with one or both. Then, over time, the power of the CSU identity in San Jose would be allowed to emerge. The school should then have an easier time attracting more traditional-age, residential students who are more likely to support the school after they graduate.

Restoration of the original California State identity in San Jose would also have a beneficial impact on the greater CSU system. As the founding Cal State campus becomes better known and regarded, the whole system would be lifted. Perhaps other campuses like Fresno State would also go over to more state-oriented identities. The CSU brand would become more prestigious and would be coveted instead of rejected and covered up as it is now at San Jose State and some other campuses.

Perhaps the first step to CSU restoration at San Jose State should be to restore the kind of "alternate identity" that already exists at CSU Long Beach/Long Beach State. That would be an important initial step toward seeing the school benefit from its original identity. To achieve such a goal, the California State Alumni Association has developed a program for gradual CSU reform and restoration at San Jose State. Far from being just a name change, this platform includes the following provisions:

(1) Reform the CSU system and San Jose State by (a) restoring the words "California State University" as a part of the founding campus identity while maintaining a strong San Jose identity, and (b) restoring the freedom of speech and association of San Jose State students and alumni to use the CSU identity, organize in support of it, and purchase associated merchandise.

(2) Restore the legislated and authentic May 2, 1862, date of establishment of the CSU and its San Jose campus,

(3) Restore the Great Seal of California as an important symbol of the founding Cal State campus in San Jose.

(4) Protect and preserve the history of the California State Normal School and CSU San Jose, and discontinue the policies that seek to hide the school's original identity.

(5) (a) Restore the original mission of the founding California State campus in San Jose to be a statewide institution representing every county in the state, and (b) raise academic standards by discontinuing any preference for locals who cannot meet the same minimum standards non-locals must meet.

SUMMARY AND CONCLUSION

11

The story of California State started with its name, derived from the fictional island of California, a paradise inspired by Greek legends of Amazon warriors who used golden implements. It echoes the story of America and the struggle to escape the tyranny of absolute monarchies and religions that sought to dominate all aspects of life. The state of California was born of rebellions and upheavals—first by Mexico to achieve independence from Spain, then by the Mexican government to secularize the missions, and later by Californians of different backgrounds rising up against the corrupt and distant Mexican government.

After joining the United States, California sought to keep pace with other states by founding the California State Normal School as its first statewide institution of higher learning. The original California State campus later found a permanent home in San Jose and spawned other campuses that would evolve into the California State University system. In 1887, however, the same year the cornerstone for Stanford University was laid by a powerful U.S. Senator and former California governor, the word "California" was stripped from the identity of those schools, leaving them vaguely identified as "State Normal Schools."

Despite this setback, the original California State institution of higher learning in San Jose remained steeped in state identity, including continued use of the California State name in school publications; its blue, gold and white colors; and its version of the Great Seal of California. Later the Spartan identity was added, furthering the same classical Greek-Roman themes found in the name California and in the school's version of the Great Seal.

Over the years, however, the loss of the word California took its toll on the older campuses and the state schools in San Jose, San Diego, and elsewhere began to be known by the name of their home city plus the word "State." At San Jose State, supporters of that identity accelerated this process in the 1950s by changing the school's year of establishment, revising its history, and mislabeling historical images and artifacts. Later the school's Great Seal was also abandoned. Founded as a statewide institution to represent every county in the state, the founding Cal State campus devolved into a provincial city-state campus primarily serving commuter students from San Jose area.

Meanwhile, California itself grew ever more well-known and popular. Already a global entertainment and tourism power, it spawned the Silicon Valley technology industry. As in the days of the Californios and the California Republic, a kind of California state nationalism still thrives. California remains a top destination for people moving from within and without the United States and has become a worldwide cultural phenomenon, celebrated in countless books, songs, and movies. While others poured into the state and celebrated its name, San Jose State supporters chose instead to hide their school's epic connection with the state.

Then in 1972, when the California State Colleges became the California State University, the state attempted to rectify its earlier mistake and restore a unified Cal State identity to its state university campuses. This effort included a modernized version of San Jose's original name: California State University, San Jose. But city-state provincialism had already taken hold at the older campuses and five of them circumvented traditional campus procedures and went straight to the legislature to restore their provincial identities.

The obvious value of the California connection was not lost on all CSU students, alumni, and educators however. At Long Beach, Sacramento, and Fresno, educators and others fought to retain some vestige of a Cal State identity. Even at San Jose State, the most stalwart of the city-state campuses, a movement sprung up in 2003 to restore the school's historic California State connection. In 2007, 25 percent of students voted to restore the school's CSU identity, despite a campaign by both administrators and some students to derail and then defeat the initiative.

In 2011, the California State Alumni Association, representing thousands of alumni and students, applied to become a chapter of the SJSU alumni association. However, the application was rejected because the official alumni group still wants to focus on building the San Jose-only identity.

Nonetheless, after almost forty years of that identity, only 6 percent of alumni have bothered to join the SJSU-only alumni group. Moreover, the school, its students, and graduates continue to struggle with mediocre regional academic rankings, poor reviews by students and alumni, and anemic attendance at major sporting events. These statistics prove that for the majority of SJSU alumni, the school engenders little more than apathy.

Instead of focusing on what's best for students and alumni, San Jose State supporters choose to focus on differentiating the founding Cal State campus from other, mostly small and distant CSU campuses. They denounce the CSU restoration movement as just a name change movement. Despite SJSU's claims to encourage diversity, San Jose State supporters continue to push a culturally narrow identity on all students and alumni. To buttress this identity, they have unlawfully changed the school's year of establishment, changed the school's name without a vote, discarded its most ancient symbols, and even reached back in time to rewrite its history. While giving lip service to diversity, they block any attempt at reform and exclude CSU-oriented students and alumni from participation in school institutions.

The SJSU Alumni Association accepts state resources while encouraging policies that engender a culture under which the California State name is suppressed and even despised. These policies receive de facto support from officials at the CSU chancellor's office, whose policies and initiatives favor the mostly Southern California campuses from which they hail.

For these reasons, the California State Alumni Association was founded and has waged an almost ten-year struggle to free the original California State campus from the provincialism and mediocrity of San Jose city-statism. The CSAA represents students and alumni who seek the right to maximize the value of their degrees by exploiting the CSU identity. They view being able to do so as an important freedom of speech and association issue, and see a CSU-branded degree as a property right paid for by their tuition and taxes.

Instead of focusing on differentiating the school from a few small and distant CSU campuses, CSU-oriented alumni believe the school should focus on competing with bigger campuses with similar histories like UC Berkeley, Oregon State, Washington State, Nevada, and Arizona State. Moreover, San Jose's powerful California State identity evokes not only the grandeur of the great state of California, but also a powerful history and symbols like the Great Seal and its goddess Minerva/Athena, from which the Spartan identity likely sprang. These symbols, like the name California itself, evoke themes from classical antiquity as a secular counterweight to the school's provincial and quasi-religious San Jose identity.

CSU-oriented alumni do not disparage San Jose's Spanish heritage and do not want to change the name of the city itself or get rid of their school's city identity. These alumni, who come from many cultural backgrounds, simply believe that a more balanced identity that includes *both* the school's state and city identities would be more equitable and beneficial for all students and alumni. After all, the word California also has a Spanish background.

But these alumni espouse much more than just a name change; they envision a paradigm shift in orientation and policies away from city-state provincialism and mediocrity. CSU alumni in San Jose seek a better Cal State campus that benefits all students and alumni, as well as the broader CSU system and the state of California. They believe the City of San Jose would also benefit greatly from such changes. To achieve this goal, the CSAA continues to work for California State historic preservation in San Jose and beyond and for the rights of students and alumni to market their education under the name on our degrees: the California State University, San Jose.

Part of that work is the publication of this book, the first half of which is intended to stand as a historically accurate portrayal of San Jose's California State heritage. It is hoped this will counteract the historical revisionism perpetrated by San Jose State supporters, much of it funded by California State taxpayer dollars. It is the goal of the CSAA and of this book to make San Jose State and the broader CSU system a place where the words "California State" are respected and coveted instead of despised and hidden. After all, as Gilbert and Burdick said, San Jose is not a state.

BIBLIOGRAPHY

"2011/2012 Philanthropic Annual Report." *The California State University*. Accessed April 24, 2013. http://www.calstate.edu/universityadvancement/reports/1112philanthropicsupport/documents/PhilanthropicReport2011-2012-FINAL.pdf.

Allen, Charles H. *Historical Sketch of the State Normal School at San Jose: 1862–1889*. Sacramento: J.D. Young, Supt. of State Printing, 1889.

"America's Favorite Cities 2012." *Travel + Leisure Magazine*. (2012.) Accessed May 10, 2013. http://www.travelandleisure.com/americas-favorite-cities/2012.

"An Act…Relating to the State Normal Schools or Teachers Colleges." In *Statutes of California*, 471–473. Sacramento: State Printing Office, 1921.

"An Act…Related to the California State University and Colleges." In *Statutes of California*, 873–874. Sacramento: State of California, 1973.

"An Act…Relating to State Colleges." In *Statutes of California*, 948–949. Sacramento: George H. Moore, State Printer, 1935.

"An Act…Relating to the Organization, Powers and Duties of Boards of Trustees of the State Normal Schools." In *Statutes of California*, 136–139. Sacramento: P. L. Shoaff, Supt. State Printing, 1887.

"An Act to Establish a Branch State Normal School." In *Statutes of California*, 12. Sacramento: State Printing Office, 1881.

"An Act to Establish a State Normal School." In *Statutes of California*, 789–91. Sacramento: D. W. Gelwicks, State Printer, 1870.

"An Act to Establish and Maintain a State Normal School." In *The Statutes of California*, 472–473. Sacramento: Benj. P. Avery, State Printer, 1862.

Barber, Nigel. "Is Sport a Religion? Sport is Replacing Religion." *Pyschology Today*, November 11, 2009. Accessed April 24, 2013. http://www.psychologytoday.com/blog/the-human-beast/200911/is-sport-religion.

Bernthal, Craig. "Declarative Consultation and the New Fresno State Logo." *Huron Country Extract*. April 18, 2012. Accessed April 23, 2013. http://huroncountyextract.blogspot.com/2012/04/0-false-18-pt-18-pt-0-0-false-false.html.

"Best Colleges. 2013." *U. S. News and World Report*. 2013. Accessed May 11, 2013. http://colleges.usnews.rankingsandreviews.com/best-colleges.

Cal State Online. 2013. Accessed May 10, 2013. http://www.calstateonline.com/cso/home/index.

California State Normal School. *California State Normal School Bulletin 1918–1919.* Sacramento: State Priting Office, 1918.

"Cal State Sacramento Going to CSU Board for Name Change." *Spartan Daily,* February 22, 2005. Accessed April 23, 2013. http://spartandaily.com/55964/cal-state-sacramento-going-to-csu-board-for-name-change

Chandler, Robert J. *California: An Illustrated History.* New York: Hippocrene Books, 2004.

Crimmins, Bob. "A Historic Pictorial of the Leland Stanford Connection." *Living in the West,* (July 2012): 19–21.

"CSU-SJ Name Change Fails. *Spartan Daily,* March 22, 2007. Accessed May 8, 2013, http://spartandaily.com/57912/csu-sj-name-change-fails.

Gerth, Donald R. and James O. Haehn. *An Invisible Giant: The California State Colleges.* San Francisco: Jossey-Bass, 1971.

Gilbert, Benjamin. *Pioneers for One Hundred Years: San Jose State College 1857–1957.* San Jose: San Jose State College, 1957.

— and Charles Burdick. *Washington Square 1857–1889: The History of San Jose State University.* San Jose: San Jose State University, 1979.

"California State University San Jose" *Google Search Results.* Accessed May 10, 2013, https://www.google.com/search?sourceid=navclient&aq=&oq=percent22california+

state+universitypercent2C+san+josepercent22&ie=UTF-8&rlz=1T4GZAG_enUS431US431&q=percent22california+state+universitypercent2C+san+josepercent22&gs_l=hp...0l5.0.0.0.9911...........0.2WgG9XyKafA#rlz=1T4GZAG_enUS431US4.

Greathead, Sarah Estelle Hammond. *The Story of an Inspiring Past: Historical Sketch of the San José State Teachers College from 1862 to 1928.* San Jose: State Teachers College at San Jose, 1928.

Hall, Frederic. *The History of San Jose and Surroundings.* San Francisco: A.L. Bancroft and Company, 1871.

"Historic Milestones." *The California State University.* April 12, 2012. Accessed April 5, 2013. http://www.calstate.edu/PA/info/milestones.shtml.

Krieger, Lisa M. "SJSU Students Try to Change School Name to Boost Prestige." *San Jose Mercury News.* March 1, 2007. Accessed May 8, 2013. http://www.mercurynews.com/search/ci_5329168.

Moon, Danelle, and Annette Nellen. "From "Minn's Evening Normal School" to "SJSU" 1857–2007." San Jose: San Jose State University Special Collections, 2007.

Pew Research Center Forum on Religion & Public Life. "'No Religion' on the Rise: 19.6 percent Have No Religious Affiliation." *The Pew Forum.* October 9, 2012. Accessed April 2, 2013, http://www.pewforum.org/Unaffiliated/nones-on-the-rise.aspx.

"San Jose State University." *U. S News and World Report.* Accessed April 25, 2013.

http://colleges.usnews.rankingsandreviews.com/best-colleges/san-jose-state-university-1155.

"San Jose State University." *Yelp.* 2013. Accessed May 11, 2013. http://www.yelp.com.

Schevitz, Tanya. *Sam Jose Students Hope to Add CSU to University Name.* SFGate. March 12, 2007. Accessed May 8, 2013. http://www.sfgate.com/education/article/SAN-JOSE-Students-hope-to-add-CSU-to-university-2611218.php.

"SJSU Centennial Materials Collection." *University Special Collections.* San Jose: San Jose State University, 1956–1962.

"SJSU Traditions." *San Jose State University.* June 2, 2006. Accessed April 12, 2013. http://www.cob.sjsu.edu/nellen_a/traditions.htm.

"Sober Living Homes" *Spartan Daily.* May 9, 2013. Accessed May 14, 2013.

http://spartandaily.com/105708/sober-living-homes.

Starr, Kevin. *California: A History.* New York: Modern Library, 2005.

"Board of Trustees – Overview." *The California State University-Board of Trustees.* June 5, 2012. Accessed May 8, 2013. http://www.calstate.edu/bot/overview.shtml.

"The Founding of Arizona State University." *ASU Libraries.* December 2001. Accessed April 5, 2010. http://www.asu.edu/lib/archives/asustory/intro.htm.

"Timeline." *San Jose State University.* April 29, 2012. Accessed May 16, 2013. http://www.sjsu.edu/about_sjsu/history/timeline/.U.S. News & World Report. *Best Colleges.*

2013. http://colleges.usnews.rankingsandreviews.com/best-colleges (accessed April 27, 2013).

UC Regents. *19th Century-Founding UC's Flagship Campus.* 2013. Accessed April 5, 2013. http://www.berkeley.edu/about/hist/foundations.shtml.

Wahlquist, John T. "San Jose State College-Nine Decades of Serivce." In *The California State Colleges: A Series of Articles Reprinted from California Schools: Volume XXV, 1954.* edited by State Dept. of Education, 25–36. Sacramento: State Dept. of Education, 1955.

Wikipedia contributors, "List of Popular Place Names." *Wikipedia.* April 27, 2013. Accessed May 10, 2013. http://en.wikipedia.org/wiki/List_of_popular_place_names.

Wikipedia contributors, "San Jose State Spartans Football Team." *Wikipedia.* January 7, 2013. Accessed April 23, 2013. http://en.wikipedia.org/wiki/2012_San_Jose_State_Spartans_football_team.

Williams, David, and Warren Beck. *California: A History of the Golden State.* New York: Doubleday, 1972.

NOTES

1. Robert Chandler, *California: An Illustrated History* (New York: Hippocrene Books, 2004), 13.

2. Frederic Hall, *The History of San Jose and Surroundings* (San Francisco: A.L. Bancroft and Company, 1871), 19.

3. Kevin Starr, *California: A History* (New York: Modern Library, 2005), 40–41.

4. David Williams, and Warren Beck, *California: A History of the Golden State* (New York: Doubleday, 1972), 73.

5. "The Founding of Arizona State University," *ASU Libraries*. December 2001. Accessed April 5, 2010. http://www.asu.edu/lib/archives/asustory/intro.htm.

6. "An Act to Establish and Maintain a State Normal School," in *The Statutes of California*, (Sacramento: Benj. P. Avery, State Printer, 1862), 472–473.

7. "An Act to Establish a State Normal School," in *Statutes of California*, (Sacramento: D. W. Gelwicks, State Printer, 1870), 789–791.

8. Benjamin Gilbert, and Charles Burdick, *Washington Square 1857–1889: The History of San Jose*

State University (San Jose: San Jose State University, 1979), 22.

9. Wahlquist, John T, "San Jose State College - Nine Decades of Service," in *The California State Colleges: A Series of Articles Reprinted from California Schools: Volume XXV, 1954,* edited by State Dept. of Education, (Sacramento: State Dept. of Education, 1955), 25.

10. Charles H. Allen, *Sketch of the State Normal School at San Jose: 1862–1889*, (Sacramento: J.D. Young, Supt. of State Printing, 1889), 67.

11. "An Act to Establish a Branch State Normal School," in *Statutes of California*, (Sacramento: State Printing Office, 1881).

12. "An Act...Relating to the Organization, Powers and Duties of Boards of Trustees of the State Normal Schools," in *Statutes of California*, (Sacramento: P. L. Shoaff, Supt. State Printing, 1887), 136–139.

13. Bob Crimmins, "A Historic Pictorial of the Leland Stanford Connection," *Living in the West*, (July 2012), 20.

14. California State Normal School, *California State Normal School Bulletin 1918–1919,* (Sacramento: State Priting Office, 1918).

15. "An Act...Relating to the State Normal Schools or Teachers Colleges," In *Statutes of California*, (Sacramento: State Printing Office, 1921), 471–473.

16. "SJSU Traditions," *San Jose State University,* June 2, 2006, accessed April 12, 2013. http://www.cob.sjsu.edu/nellen_a/traditions.htm.

17   Sarah Estelle Hammond Greathead, *The Story of an Inspiring Past: Historical Sketch of the San José State Teachers College from 1862 to 1928* (San Jose: State Teachers College at San Jose, 1928), 68, 84.

18.   "An Act…Relating to State Colleges," in *Statutes of California*, (Sacramento: George H. Moore, State Printer, 1935), 948–949.

19.   *The California State University - Board of Trustees*, June 5, 2012, accessed May 8, 2013, http://www.calstate.edu/bot/overview.shtml.

20   Danelle Moon, and Annette Nellen, "From 'Minn's Evening Normal School' to 'SJSU' 1857–2007," (San Jose: University Special Collections, 2007).

21.   "SJSU Centennial Materials Collection," *University Special Collections*, (San Jose: San Jose State University, 1956–1962).

22.   UC Regents, *19th Century - Founding UC's Flagship Campus.* 2013, accessed April 5, 2013. http://www.berkeley.edu/about/hist/foundations.shtml.

23   Benjamin Gilbert, *Pioneers for One Hundred Years: San Jose State College 1857–1957*, (San Jose: San Jose State College, 1957), 82.

24.   *The California State University-Board of Trustees*, June 5, 2012, accessed May 8, 2013,

http://www.calstate.edu/bot/overview.shtml.

25.   "An Act…Related to the California State University and Colleges," in *Statutes of California*, (Sacramento: State of California, 1973), 873–874.

26 Benjamin Gilbert, and Charles Burdick, *Washington Square 1857–1889: The History of San Jose State University,* (San Jose: San Jose State University, 1979), 196.

27. "An Act…Related to the California State University and Colleges," in *Statutes of California,* (Sacramento: State of California, 1973), 873–874.

28. Bernthal, Craig, *Declarative Consultation and the New Fresno State Logo,* April 18, 2012, accessed April 23, 2013. http://huroncountyextract.blogspot.com/2012/04/0-false-18-pt-18-pt-0-0-false-false.html.

29. "Cal State Sacramento Going to CSU Board for Name Change," *Spartan Daily,* February 22, 2005, accessed April 23, 2013, http://spartandaily.com/55964/cal-state-sacramento-going-to-csu-board-for-name-change.

30. Schevitz, Tanya, *San Jose Students Hope to Add CSU to University Name,* SFGate. March 12, 2007, accessed May 8, 2013. http://www.sfgate.com/education/article/SAN-JOSE-Students-hope-to-add-CSU-to-university-2611218.php.

31 Krieger, Lisa M., *SJSU Students Try to Change School Name to Boost Prestige,* March 1, 2007 , accessed May 8, 2013, http://www.mercurynews.com/search/ci_5329168.

32. "CSU-SJ Name Change Fails." *Spartan Daily,* March 22, 2007, accessed May 8, 2013,

http://spartandaily.com/57912/csu-sj-name-change-fails.

33. "Timeline." *San Jose State University.* April 29, 2012, accessed May 16, 2013. http://www.sjsu.edu/

about_sjsu/history/timeline/.U.S. News & World Report. *Best Colleges.* 2013. http://colleges.usnews.rankingsandreviews.com/best-colleges (accessed April 27, 2013).

34. *The California State University-Board of Trustees,* June 5, 2012, accessed May 8, 2013, http://www.calstate.edu/bot/overview.shtml

35 Donald R. Gerth, and James O. Haehn. *An Invisible Giant: The California State Colleges,* (San Francisco: Jossey-Bass, 1971).

36. *Cal State Online,* 2013, accessed May 10, 2013, http://www.calstateonline.com/cso/home/index.

37. "California State University San Jose," *Google Search Results,* accessed May 10, 2013, https://www.google.com/search?sourceid=navclient&aq=&oq=percent22california+state+universitypercent2C+san+josepercent22&ie=UTF-8&rlz=1T4GZAG_enUS431US431&q=percent22california+state+universitypercent2C+san+josepercent22&gs_l=hp...0l5.0.0.0.9911...........0.2WgG9XyKafA#rlz=1T4GZAG_enUS431US4.

38. " America's Favorite Cities 2012," *Travel + Leisure Magazine,* (2012), accessed May 10, 2013, http://www.travelandleisure.com/americas-favorite-cities/2012.

39. Wikipedia contributors, "List of Popular Place Names." *Wikipedia.* April 27, 2013. Accessed May 10, 2013. http://en.wikipedia.org/wiki/List_of_popular_place_names.

40. "San Jose State University," *U. S News and World Report,* Accessed April 25, 2013,

http://colleges.usnews.rankingsandreviews.com/
best-colleges/san-jose-state-university-1155.

41. Wikipedia contributors, "San Jose State
Spartans Football Team." *Wikipedia*. January 7, 2013.
Accessed April 23, 2013.
http://en.wikipedia.org/
wiki/2012_San_Jose_State_Spartans_football_team.

42. "Sober Living Homes," *Spartan Daily*, May 9,
2013, accessed May 14, 2013,

http://spartandaily.com/105708/sober-living-homes.

43. Pew Research Center Forum on Religion & Public
Life, "'No Religion' on the Rise: 19.6 percent Have No
Religious Affiliation," *The Pew Forum*. October 9, 2012,
accessed April 2, 2013, http://www.pewforum.org/
Unaffiliated/nones-on-the-rise.aspx.

44. Barber, Nigel. "Is Sport a Religion? Sport is
Replacing Religion," *Pyschology Today*, November 11,
2009, accessed April 24, 2013, http://www.psychologyto-
day.com/blog/the-human-beast/200911/is-sport-religion.

45. "San Jose State University." *Yelp*. 2013, accessed
May 11, 2013, http://www.yelp.com.

46. *The California State University - Board of Trustees,*
June 5, 2012, accessed May 8, 2013,

http://www.calstate.edu/bot/overview.shtml.

47. "San Jose State University," *U. S News and
World Report*. Accessed April 25, 2013, http://col-
leges.usnews.rankingsandreviews.com/best-colleges/
san-jose-state-university-1155.

IMAGE CREDITS

Note: As described in this book, San Jose State University routinely mislabels California State Normal School historical items as being from the "San Jose State Normal School," which was never an official name of the school. In the following image credits the mislabeled names are used to assist others in finding these materials, and where necessary in the interest of accuracy a historically correct name is also provided.

Figure 1 – "Students Outside of San Jose State Normal School," photograph, 1870, *San Jose State University Archives Photograph Collection, http://digitalcollections.sjlibrary.org/cdm/singleitem/collection/sjsuUA/id/643/rec/27* (accessed August 4, 2013). Historically Accurate Title: "Students Outside California State Normal School Building."

Figure 2 – [State Normal School at San Jose Great Seal Logo from the 1910 Degree of Georgia F. Gardner], photograph, 2012, *San Jose State University Archives.*

Figure 3 – "San Jose State Normal School Football Team Players," photograph, 1900-06, *San Jose State University Archives Photograph Collection, http://digitalcollections.sjlibrary.org/cdm/singleitem/collection/sjsuUA/*

id/1196/rec/55 (accessed August 4, 2013).Historically Accurate Title:"State Normal School at San Jose Football Team Players."

Figure 4 – [California State Normal School at San Jose Catalog 1904], photograph, 2012, *San Jose State University Archives.*

Figure 5 – "Men's Basketball Team," photograph, 1910, *San Jose State University Archives Photograph Collection, http://digitalcollections.sjlibrary.org/cdm/singleitem/collection/ sjsuUA/id/870/rec/46* (accessed August 4, 2013).

Figure 6 – [Cover of the California State University, San Jose, Graduate Catalog 1972/74], photograph, 2012, *San Jose State University Archives.*

Figure 7 – [San Jose State – California State University Graphic Created for 2007 CSU Alternate Identity Initiative], graphic, 2007, *California State Alumni Association Archives.*

Figure 8 – [California State Normal School Bell at San Jose State in 2005], photograph, 2005, *California State Alumni Association Archives.*

Figure 9 – [Cal State University, San Jose and San Jose State College 1862 Pennants], photograph, 2012, *San Jose State University Archives.*

Figure 10 – [San Jose State University Great Seal of California Seal from Tower Hall in 2004], photograph, 2004, *California State Alumni Association Archives.*

ABOUT THE AUTHOR

Michael Harold, a native of Toronto, Canada, is a former professional journalist and practicing attorney who currently lives in the San Francisco Bay Area and makes his living as a Director of Marketing. A lifelong history enthusiast, Mr. Harold holds a BA in political science and economics from the University of North Carolina at Chapel Hill, a Juris Doctor from American University Washington College of Law in Washington, DC, and a master's of business administration from the California State University, San Jose.

Made in the USA
San Bernardino, CA
14 March 2014